BOOK 1

~ MR. A. PRESENTS ~

FIRST SHOWSTOPPERS!

6 Impressive Late Elementary Piano Solos

DENNIS ALEXANDER

Every student likes to perform something that is sure to impress an audience. It doesn't necessarily have to be loud and fast; humor, unusual rhythms, wide ranges and unexpected sounds can also be highly successful with students and audiences alike! This collection of six entertaining and impressive-sounding late elementary solos has all of the above.

Students who like to play loud and fast will have great fun with "Boogie on Down" and "Brave Spirit Dancer." Those who like big sounds will love "Mighty Mandarin" and "Trumpeters Three." If humor is their cup of tea, "Two-Steppin' Toads" will be a favorite. And for those who are intrigued by the unusual and contemporary, "Neanderthal" will pique their curiosity!

All of these pieces are designed for students with small hands, and each piece explores a wide range of the keyboard. If you're looking for music that will motivate your students to practice more, you'll enjoy this sparkling collection of *First Showstoppers!* Best wishes.

Dennis Alexander

D0608165

This collection is dedicated to my friend and colleague Dennis Thurmond.

Cover art: Shawn McKelvey • Cover design: Tanya Maiboroda
Music engraving: Nancy Butler • Art direction: Ted Engelbart

About ~ MR. A. PRESENTS ~

A few years ago, some of my piano students at the University of Montana decided that it would be much easier to refer to me as "Mr. A." Needless to say, I agreed that "Mr. A." would be less work, both in pronunciation and written form. Consequently, when coming up with a title for this new series of books, I decided that "Mr. A. Presents" would be the perfect way to introduce this new identity to all of you.

Boogie on Down

Dennis Alexander

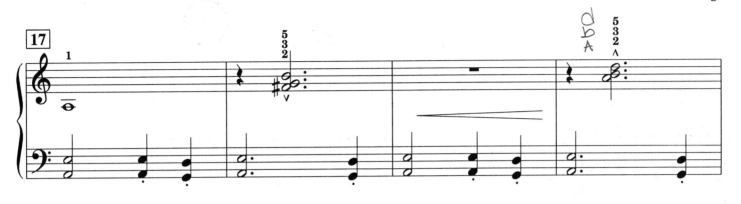

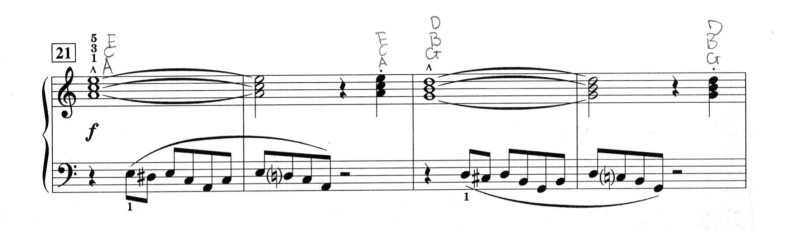

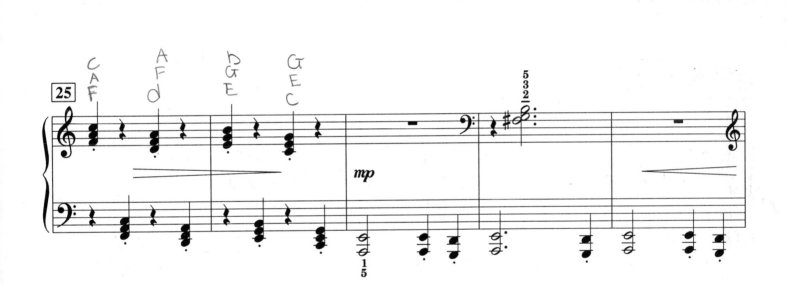

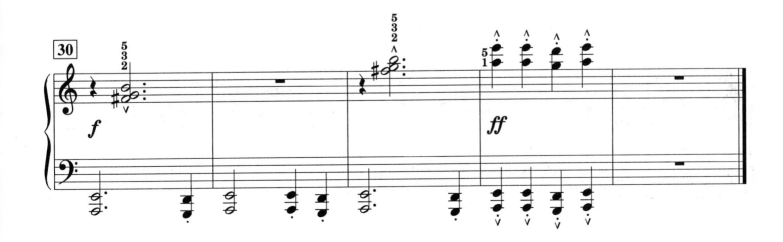

Trumpeters Three

With vigor! ($\textstyle \frac{}{} = 80$)

Dennis Alexander

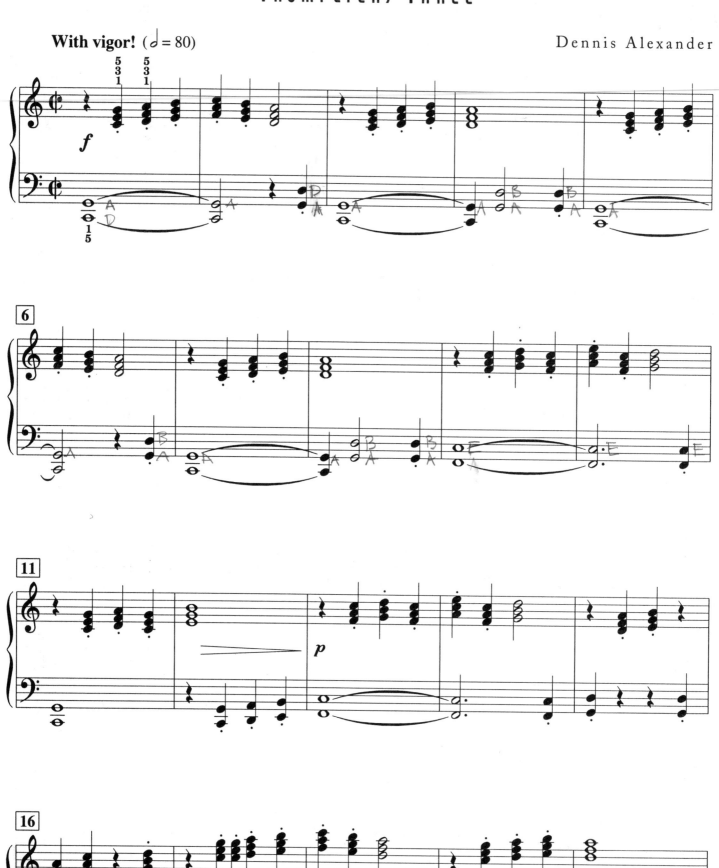

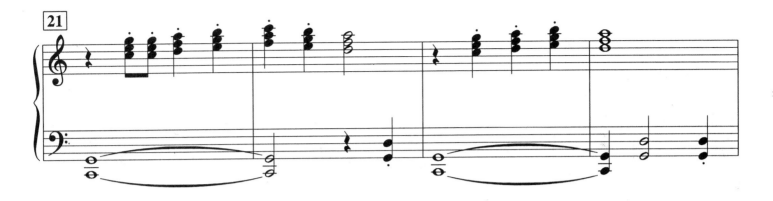

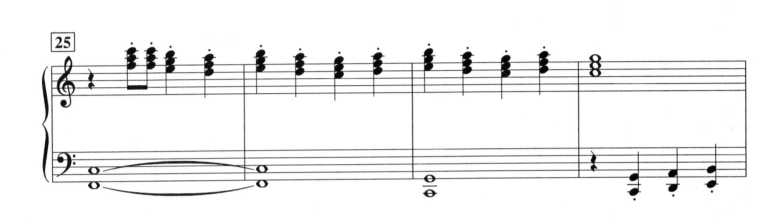

Two-Steppin' Toads

Dennis Alexander

With humor (♩ = 152)

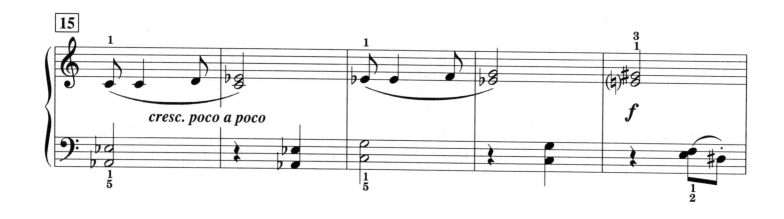

Brave Spirit Dancer

Dennis Alexander

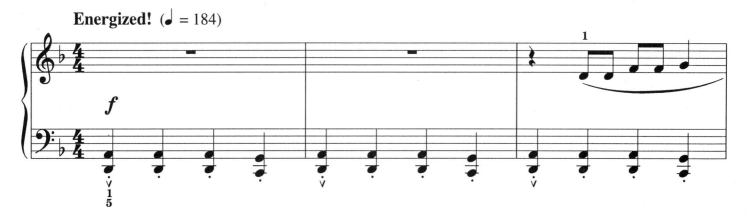

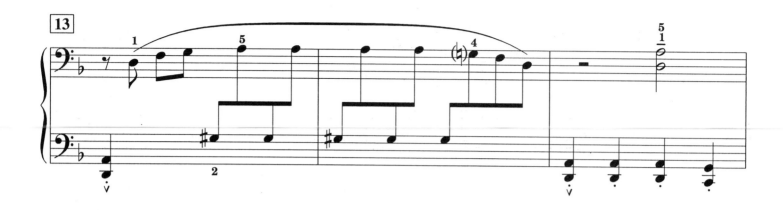

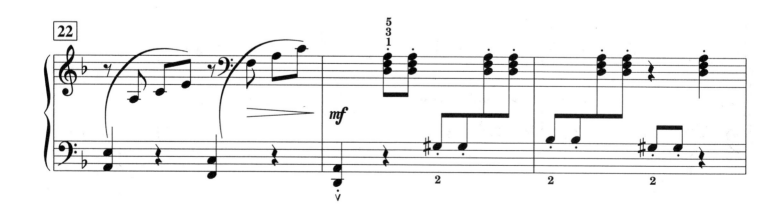

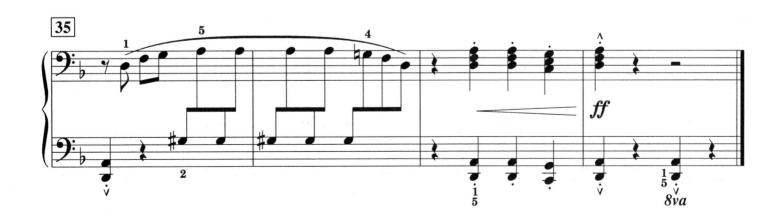

Mighty Mandarin

Dennis Alexander

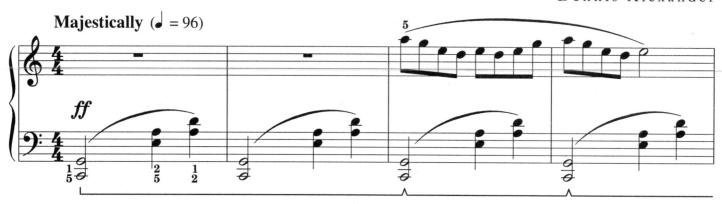

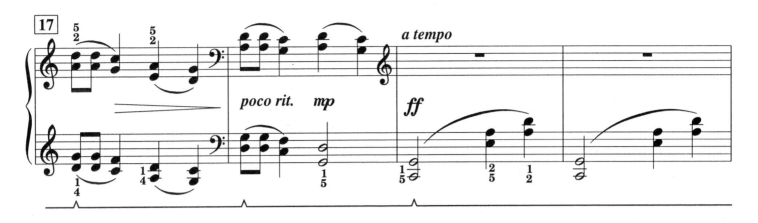

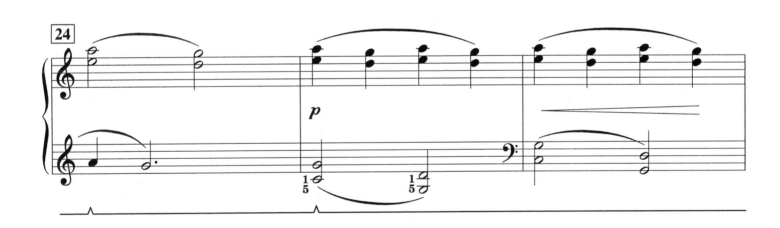

Neanderthal

*Let your imagination soar as you wander through
this prehistoric musical journey!*

Dennis Alexander

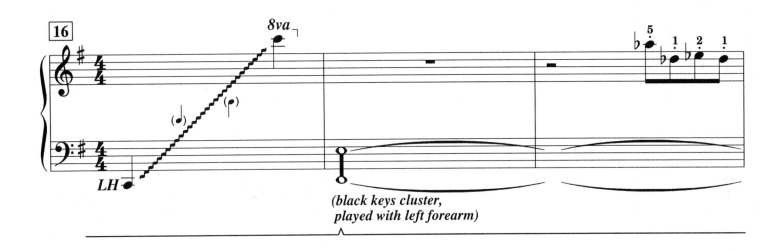

(black keys cluster,
played with left forearm)

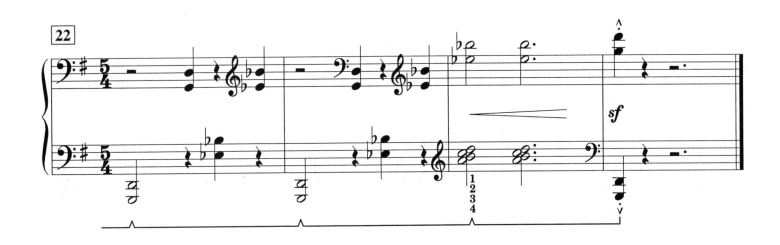